SECOND INNOCENCE

Poems by Guy Reed

Luchador Press
Big Tuna, TX

Copyright © Guy Reed, 2020
First Edition1 3 5 7 9 10 8 6 4 2
ISBN: 978-1-950380-83-1
LCCN: 202090122

Design, edits and layout: El Dopa
Cover and title page image: Hannah Jensen
Author photo: Kelly Sinclair
All rights reserved. No part of this publication may be reproduced or transmitted in any form or by any means, electronic or mechanical, including photocopying, recording or by info retrieval system, without prior written permission from the author.

Acknowledgements:

Poetry East — Astonishment, Bat Dream

Green Kill Gallery Broadside — Ashes, Why I Don't Write Like Frank O'Hara, also collected in the chapbook, *Until The Words Came*, Post Traumatic Press, 2019.

Home Planet News — Conveyance Object #4 (as Blue Conveyance)

Calling All Poets Anthology, 2015 CAPS Press. Marina Mati, ed. — 1963 Evinrude

Lifeblood; Woodstock Poetry Society Anthology, 2011, Chickaree Press. Trina Porte, ed. — Euphoria In Ohio

Collected in the chapbook, *The Effort To Hold Light*, 2011, Finishing Line Press — Americana, Conveyance Object #4, Copper Memories, Husks, October Gray, Seeing The Starry Night

TABLE OF CONTENTS

I

Apples / 1

Husks / 2

My Savior / 4

No. 16 (Red, Brown, and Black), 1958 / 5

Leaping Deer / 7

Patience / 10

Euphoria in Ohio / 11

Seeing *The Starry Night* / 13

Skylights / 15

Ashes / 16

Alfred Delphin Bresson, Born 1894 / 17

1963 Evinrude / 19

One Year After / 22

Americana / 23

The Iron House / 26

II

A Bomb Went off in Your Ocean / 31

What Memories Are Carried in Light? / 33

April / 36

October Gray / 37

Nice Clothes / 39

Copper Memories / 42

It Is the Fourth of July, Again / 43

Long-Legged Blond / 45

What I Wish / 46

Shared Burden / 49

To Know the Difference / 50

Last Melt / 52

Conveyance Object #4, 1976-1977 / 53

III

What I Wanted to Tell You / 57

Why I Don't Write Like Frank O'Hara / 58

Acceptance / 59

Invisible / 60

Faith / 61

The Hands of My Mother / 63

Second Influence / 65

What Was Left at the End / 66

Maybe in My Eyes / 67

Astonishment / 68

Bat Dream / 69

Air Travel / 70

Surviving / 71

Prayer / 74

Asher, Bresson, Horton, Reed, for the folks

Had I the heavens' embroidered cloths,
Enwrought with golden and silver light,
The blue and the dim and the dark cloths
Of night and light and the half-light...

-W.B. Yeats

I

Apples

I pack a fresh home-grown apple
into my daughter's brown bag lunch. Six
weeks into high school, her mornings have
more make-up and the bus stop now
at the end of the country lane.
We rush to wait in the car,
listen to music or the weather;
some mornings we're foggy or grumpy
or like today, silent. She's grown long legs,
has the same large hazel eyes. Her hair
is blond and purple. She wears black boots.
Backpack on shoulders, books held in folded
arms— she glides onto the bus with ease.
Mutsu apples, yellow-green with a rose
blush, lie still under the trees in the
brown grass of October. Dew
sheen on their skin in the amber
light of early morning. The ground will
swallow these sweet globes— autumn's truth
at the end of spring's promise. These trees
bear fruit every other year, no choice
but patience. The sun continues to glow,
but the warmth has gone south, leaving
a trail of gold, which will fade to white
and then gray long before school bells are
silenced again for summer. The apple
placed on the teacher's desk, fairytale
left behind, when time was something
we were busy learning how to keep.

Husks

My father fed the birds,
his second-floor balcony, about which
the first-floor tenant complained,
husks floating her way. A friend
made a tray with sides and a screen
to contain what the sparrows

left behind. What my father left behind
was chirping birds at the sliding glass doors.
Where is he? they seemed to ask,
tilting their heads. Four winters
they depended on him to pull them
through. Here in November the food
has dwindled again. I wasn't sure

how to tell the sparrows, perched
around the balcony railing, that my father
was gone, that they needed to find
his soul, release it from its egg,
raise it in the nest and teach
it to fly. To find another
who sets out seed to help the small
birds survive the season
of cold absence. These glass doors
reflecting empty docks, the lake
soon to be frozen. Days passed,

less and less seed. The sparrows
began their day on the balcony
but stayed less and less. More
and more people came to the apartment,
then fewer and fewer until I was alone
again. Eventually, the tray had to go.
I spread the remaining seed
in the park near the kiosks
covered for the season and sat on a bench
watching the stillness of the lake,
the grayness of the wood dock,
the water, the sky. Nothing moved.

My Savior

I had lain perfectly still in the dark bedroom,
convinced if I moved even one toe,
God would instantly strike me dead.
I had just begun kindergarten.
Mother's footsteps came near enough to call out,
not too loudly lest I make a movement
and disturb God's unwavering mind and eye.
Light cut in from the hall as she entered.

*No, Honey, God would never do that
especially to a good boy like you,* she cooed
as if I were her baby bird, coaxed to its first leap
of faith. Raised a finger, then moved a hand,
I continued to breathe. Shook my sleep leaden legs
and my heart still beat.

Escaping the all-seeing, all-knowing great pain
of death, unscathed, a shudder of tears released,
I knew my mother backed God down
to save me in my footed pajamas.
Through childhood tribulations to follow,
all the years of my father's angry rants
and punishments, she had my back.
She became the New Testament.

No. 16 (Red, Brown, and Black), 1958

*a painting is not a picture of an experience,
it is an experience* – Mark Rothko, 1959.

Nearly ten feet by nearly nine on the wall it comes at me like a night terror, three rectangular, disembodied, blurred, stacked horizontal bands of color; dark red, brown, and black pulsating inside an enormous purple stain. I yield. Not my body that shrinks from its advance, inside the corridors of my flesh a body of light turns to its side, raises an arm for shield and hunches on its knees before

the propelled vision. It's just a painting on a white wall, lights of the gallery set low. I have seen other Rothko paintings. But this one grows... to engulf my soul. Yes, soul is the word I mean. I've doubted its existence, having no proof other than vague sensations in the solar plexus and this consciousness, which may only be the mind. This painting calls out my soul... fuck! Foreboding, heavy in my chest, makes it difficult to catch my breath. This threatens me. Not abstract, this is palpable, a plum hum of nightfall, Earth's shadow

circling the globe always on the hunt for light. To devour safety in what can be seen is the onslaught of blindness under a moonless night, shadows grow thick, swallow luminosity from streets and yards of even the most cheerful neighborhoods. Silence dense in unlit alleys.

This is the ancient feeling that beyond the cave-mouth fire, the darkness will eat me. My scream does not have the force to escape the black. Thankfully, a bright winter day when I stagger from the building. I survive, freighted and possibly damaged. The image continues to expand into the interior of my geometry. Nightfall fills the cracks, allows nothing to escape. Lock the door, flip the electric switch, but one cannot see into the darkness when bathed in the light, only when standing in shadow looking toward a shaft of it. I recoil from the looming shade, its dispassionate maw. I pray to again witness the break of day when hope rushes and fear recedes, genesis of edge.

Leaping Deer

I

Upstate New York, driving home in the early light,
I see to my right— motion in the field,
a deer running straight out, toward me. I brake
fast and hard knowing
it's all timed too well. All I see
out the passenger window is deer.
I scrunch for impact; a light scuffle across roof,
turn to the driver's window— deer.
It trots into the woods, stops, a doe.
She's quite large, emerging from a long,
deep snow season; she might be pregnant.
Our eyes meet each other's, she doesn't know,
backward my last name spells 'deer.'
I can't leap through the woods,
much less survive winter there. I don't
know her name that springs free and silent
through the trees. The deer and this month
of March the same colorless color of November
uncovered, with new growth underneath.
I guess we share nothing
except this crossing. She flicks her tail
and moves off as a soft rain begins to fall.

II

The phone call came early in Minnesota, nearly
five a.m. My father just died. He had been moved
to a care facility in Minneapolis. Twenty miles away in
Excelsior, I was making plans at his apartment, not
expecting that call for maybe a year. Crying, shaking,
disbelieving, I dressed.
Driving his car and talking out loud to my dad, not a
mile away an empty Highway 7. My headlights
swept the woods around Christmas Lake. In the
dark, a stag with ten-point antlers rising
into November branches, eyes reflecting light
in the pre-hunt, pre-sun dawn of the new day.
Engine idling, people and a body waiting, I left
the stag to grow trees from his regal head.

III

Our deaf neighbor driving from the opposite
direction on her way to work. I'm coming back from
the school bus stop a mile from the house. We've
passed this way before. She stopped
on the little hill, could see the wide view:
the field, the deer, my car, the woods. Witnessed
the amazing last second leap over my blue
compact. We pull up to each other slowly
with mouths open, a wide-eyed, *Wow!*, we mouth and
exclaim. Both of us lucky. Two memories
of one leap.

IV

At eight years old, I could still be an Indian brave,
running through the northern forest surrounding
my grandparents' rustic resort on Four Point Lake. I
had my trading post, eagle-headed, bone-handled, 5-
inch Bowie knife in its sheath strapped to my side
with a beaded belt. Deep in woods
with pines so thick it looked like a magnified head of
hair. I was stalking my imagination
when a herd of near twenty white-tailed deer
bolt like thunder, startled the hell out of me
with a thrill. In the August shade I watched the deer
go through a break in the trees
shine through the sunlight and disappear.
The dust billowed. I tasted it in the hazy heat.
I discovered a carcass: fur, antlers and bones. I
grabbed the antlers and took the hide,
full of worms, for a coat. I told my Grandma
that I jumped a deer, wrestled it to the ground,
skinned it and cut off the antlers. She laughed,
let me keep the bones that grew from the head.
End of vacation, I didn't want my parents
to bring me back home, to school. It would be
twenty years before I ever thought to spell
my last name backwards and rediscover
what I knew at eight. There was still time to be
anything I wanted: a guide, or the wind, an animal or
just a spirit leaping through the trees on my way to
the deeper forest where the trees
are thickest and language is unspoken.

Patience

After a year I stopped expecting the phone
to ring on Sunday evenings, didn't jump
when it rang on Wednesdays. Found
other ways to begin my Friday nights.
There have been no specters, no signs,
nothing that would make me think,
Ah, that was my father. No misty whispers,
or, *What-was-that's?* No mysterious
cloud formations, nothing in the tea leaves.

What I expected was a dream visitation.
My father appearing from the dark wood
to impart sage wisdom from beyond the veil.
I felt abandoned, surprised by his utter absence.
Where did he go?

After two years, I dreamt myself in a boat,
I felt his presence there. I was having trouble
with my task. His hands came into my frame
of view to untangle my monofilament
and bait my hook
so I could continue to fish for what is hungry
under the surface of water upon which we float.

Euphoria In Ohio

Driving home to New York from the headwaters
of the Mississippi after my father's funeral. I've spent
three weeks handling his life and after it.
I'm in his car with the last of his stuff. It's raining

like hissing, screeching *yeows* and guttural, frothing
ruffs. For miles and hours in this deluge
I'm behind an F350 truck pulling a long empty trailer.
It's nearly all I can see. I'm following his

lead at 75 mph. I'm playing country music
and we're passing everybody. It was overcast,
fog when I left Minnesota yesterday.
The same through Wisconsin. Nightfall

through Illinois. It's been raining since I woke up
in Indiana. Now, somewhere in the middle
of Ohio, in the middle of the day, the rain breaks.
The road is high on a plateau– high for Ohio–

and overhead the darkest cloud I've ever seen
like the sky was turned off. Oak leaves
float by like damaged butterflies. I've
made this drive a dozen times and nothing

looks familiar. I sit up straight. Suddenly,
I find myself happy to be here, right here in Ohio.
I don't know why; my father is dead,
the sky is ominous, and the music

is about dying young in prison. My friend,
the F350, has slowed slightly. I pull out, pass him
on the left. He pulls in behind me. Now
I'm going to take us through the rest

of this storm, the rest of this state
and the next, all the way to the Atlantic
and the end of life if I have to; I feel
that good. Of that, I am confident.

Seeing *The Starry Night*

for M.H.

This is not a fake nor a smooth print
which dazzles with enhancement,
reproduction of size. It is perhaps,
the thousandth time I've seen this image,
but it's not on a calendar, coffee mug,
t-shirt, key fob, pillow case, nor
a color plate in a fine book. No,
I turn the corner in the museum
not knowing what to expect
after the Bonnard show, but I do
not expect to come face to face
with *The Starry Night*. I am at
the Museum of Modern Art,
for the first time, and there are famous
works of art. Could I have not foreseen this?
This is not *A* Starry Night, it is
The Starry Night.

No, I cannot look. Quickly,
I turn away before I see too much.
I am not prepared for its existence
after all these years. I run to another
part of the museum, look at the floor.
This is different. Yes, I know its face
well, but not the energy of the actual.

Texture of paint and brush stroke,
a naked object on the wall. How many
millions have stood there? How many
billions have not? I will return, stand
and not fidget, I will breathe and I will
be awed. No, I do not know yet
what I will be. It might disappoint, severely.
What moved past the cypresses
of Saint-Rémy that night, I cannot know.
Vincent Van Gogh stood before a blank canvas.
I step toward the unknown.

Skylights

On a walkway over the bustle
she glimmered in the light of the airport atrium
wearing a long overcoat opened to a white blouse
and tan slacks. She had a look of 1959 lipstick
and coiffed hair, but still looked like I knew her
in 2010, only aglow, like a silver-nitrate Monet.

Mom, I called, and she smiled, meeting my eyes.
I had not seen her since she passed from this world. My
insides were floating, seeing her healthy
and happy to be traveling. I knew she played piano and
loved to sing.

I fumbled with luggage not sure whose. We hugged,
I recalled later—
or simply a hope?

To give my young, not-yet-a-mother, mother,
a fond greeting before she sets out to fly toward
her future where she becomes a nurse,
meets her husband,

where I will then come into being
and farewells will be after thoughts
with no finality.

Ashes

For eight hundred eighty-three straight mornings
I have constructed different goodbyes to you.

By the end of day my heart breaks again. The look
in your eyes as they vanished from what I'd
        always known

into dark holes gives me no rest. As if
a trapdoor suddenly opened to swallow you.

Your hand reached out and I grasped, but could not
hold whatever it is that animates from inside as it

fell from view. I was sure you hovered somewhere
in the body not hungry or thirsty, not in pain, but
        perhaps

comforted by your granddaughter whose face you
stroked only minutes before as she knelt by your
        side. Time

now for me to let go of the nothing I am holding,
the only answer I have to explain your absence.

Alfred Delphin Bresson, Born 1894

Second generation French-American, thirty years old, eats his breakfast of eggs fried in fat with a thick slab of bread before sunrise. Corn harvested, the stalk stubble left in the field to hold snow's moisture on the plains where wind is constant. The lakes are beginning to freeze, the ducks have flown, but there is a field-dressed buck in the wood shed and there is a goose for Thanksgiving.

He hears on the radio the discovery of another galaxy announced, Andromeda, confirming
the Milky Way is not the only galaxy that exists
in the deep sky. There may even be many galaxies full of stars like our own— so far away
that only a 100-inch telescope, 10,000 feet above the sea can confirm this. *What does this mean for Heaven,* he wonders?

He puts on his coat and steps outdoors in the last dark before dawn. *Maybe, there is only countless burning orbs of light?* He pauses in the barnyard to look up and take in the discovery. The clink of the milk pail echoes in the silence. *Horseless buggies everywhere, aeroplanes, telephones, electric wires being strung across the land, a wireless that can tune in Chicago and now, a giant spyglass that sees billions of stars spiraling in a distant place. Interesting,* he thinks, *maybe that's Heaven?*

*The Great War is behind us. New York, Paris, London,
I've seen those places, full of lights
and people.* Then he considers the life
of a man on a mountaintop in California
doing nothing but observing stars we cannot see.
Alfred looks across the sky, horizon to horizon. There
is a silver glow beginning in the east. *There is peace,
and the world is smaller than we thought.* He smiles.
The cows still need to be milked. He heads to the
barn. *Everybody has the stars,*
he thinks, *I have stars right here.*

1963 Evinrude

Squat, compact,
white engine hood,
gray extension ending
in a white propeller.
My dad's portable outboard motor,
nine and one-half horsepower.
1963, the engine was not cheap,
but fourteen-foot wood
and aluminum row boats
were easy to rent at the marinas.
Each spring before the ice was out
it was time for maintenance.
In the basement of the rented
house, engine on its metal stand.
Lube the crank wheel, drain
and replace the lower-unit oil,
grease the propeller shaft, new cotter pin
for the prop and a new spark plug.

My short, white-haired dad
carried its weight up the stairs,
laid that engine ever so gently
in the trunk, swaddled
in the quilted packing blanket.
Throttle arm folded
and gear side up, always.

My dad must have felt something
rare and fine to zoom across the lake,
cap brim low, a smile on his son's face,
the rush of breeze and speed. Happy
after work on those June days,
to do what he loved best with his son—
the only thing as important as
whether the fish were biting.

That engine, the same age as me,
gave me a sense of growing up
when I was allowed to run it while
sitting on my dad's lap. I loved
the rooster-tail it made, swells
of water opened like a zipper.

I was strong when I carried it to the car.
I was responsible when I laid it down,
throttle arm folded and gear side up,
always. When I attached it to the boat,
connected the gas line, primed the engine,
pulled the starter rope, I was trusted.

That Evinrude, built to last, taught
the importance of quality, of care
and freedom. Nowhere on the lake
we couldn't go, zinging off to
where the fish were– or a slow
joyride along the shore

looking at the large homes with
expansive lawns and cabin cruisers
tethered to private docks. Joy
in the wind, waves and being out
where no one could reach us.

One Year After

Bodies of water in the morning
give a serenity from the outlines
of their boundaries.

I sit beside one,
listen to water lap up
to stones and dock stanchions.
Gentle is the sound that calms.

Time becomes two great herons
rising together, going north
above the summer river.
Orange sun in those blue clouds.

Americana

The most lonely Edward Hopper paintings are the
 ones
without any people– just the architecture of space.
In those houses and buildings we know there are
 people

at certain times of the day– each going about their
 lives
muted by the hands of the artist, by the brush
 strokes
of whatever providence has placed them here, in
 our past,

in a portrait of America during a time of nice hats
 and hobos
riding the rails through the unseen scapes of
 cities; backsides
lonely in this terrain of what we take for granted.
 There's a train

behind the scene of every Edward Hopper
 painting, a locomotive
moving just out of sight or obscured by the
 landscape. In every
Edward Hopper painting there is Norman
 Rockwell painting—

*

he's out of sight of Edward who cannot see
        Norman either.
Norman is painting the two boys you do not see
        walking to the sandlot
with ball, bat, and a father's old worn GI service
        mitt they'll share.

The boys throw the occasional stone behind
        Edward's
buildings near the train tracks. The stone echoes.
        Space is silence
in Edward Hopper paintings. Space is the mind
        where the thoughts

ring around the light and bounce off the shadows.
        We wish
to have a mind as organized as an Edward Hopper
        painting.
The subjects are solitary only. Solitude in the
        harsh light

which illuminates unadorned existence. It comes
        in through the window
beyond the bustle of the street. Yet, it's not
        existence in the light,
but the light which provides existence, light as
        narrative. We could

*

take a seat there and stay all day, never want to be
    part of the daily flow. Separate,
like a still life, like a painting that captures its
    subject and never looks out,
only draws in. In Rockwell, character is narrative.
    We provide. Each of us,

a portrait waiting to be drawn for eternity's gaze.
    In America,
a Norman Rockwell inside an Edward Hopper, the
    train behind the scene,
each one casting shadows that tell the other story,
    living a life of their own.

The Iron Horse

Lou Gehrig's name stamped on a baseball bat
which runs along the backrest of a wood bench
in the vestibule of St. Peter's ALS Center.
His name also stamped onto Amyotrophic Lateral
Sclerosis. Over the years one would hear, *Lou Gehrig's
Disease,* lower one's eyes and just shake the head
knowing, with no known cause, treatment or cure,
what it spelled.
Mr. Gehrig never met my mother. On the day
she was born, he went 3 for 4 and scored 2 runs.
He won the MVP that year and the Yankees
won their first World Series without Babe Ruth.

Growing up she dreamed of birthing nine boys
to field her own baseball team. Her father played
semi-pro ball until a farm accident took the sight
from an eye. He told me, *A good pitcher can throw
a strike whenever he wants.* A large, strong man,
his heart only stopped beating at ninety-four
when he had nothing left to do. My mother
loved the Yankees, an easy thing
in the Midwest. Growing up on a farm
in the 1940's and 50's, the city of liberty
was a beacon of strength. Three years old
when Lou's consecutive-game streak ended
and only five when he passed away. Her Yankees
were the Mickey Mantle matinee idol era,
but she knew the lore of the Bronx Bombers.

*

Knowing he could no longer play ball at 36,
what did Lou believe that day in June?
At the Mayo Clinic, doctors couldn't solve
the mystery of motor neurons in mutiny.
At 74, my mother didn't believe it
when told she had the disease named after
baseball's Iron Horse. She was an iron woman
in the eyes of many: full-time job and homemaker,
left her husband and moved cross country. Now
a single grandmother delivering meals,
two choirs, and three study groups.
Just a regular life. I'm on a journey of the spirit,
she'd say. Tests, country neurologists,
second opinions and then a third opinion
confirmation— bulbar-onset ALS— less frequent and
less forgiving, though ALS forgives no one.
She believed she would heal herself. Or die. Prayer,
actualization, organic homeopathy,
she ate organic food already, what else was there?

Never referred to having ALS. Whatever it was
in her mind, she'd show them a miracle
if a higher order deemed it necessary.
Doctors advised, *Conserve energy*; stubborn,
not able to speak words well, she went as hard
as she could for 16 months, came by
once a week to cook the family dinner. Insisted,
to try out new recipes and cook old favorites.

My mother never sat in the bench at the ALS Center.
She had faith in God, herself, her two sons,
daughters-in-law she loved, two grandchildren
that meant the world. Despite the bad break,
I know she considered herself the luckiest
woman on the face of the Earth.

II

A Bomb Went Off In Your Ocean

He knew his friend was right.

The shockwave had yet to surface
and the fallout would follow.

This will obliterate me,
megatons of TNT
right to the chest, he realized
while driving the car,
but I can take it.

Break it down,
element
by particle,
a multitude from one,
every atom
will sting
one at a time.
Sink the ocean floor
two thousand feet in a second,
the void of loss…

and then the tsunami…
every drop. How many at once,
one hundred?

No, one thousand—
no, the ten thousand
individual droplets at a time
until the tsunami passes through.

No way around it.

The wave rises,
shifting sand
from the bottom of the sea

and he at the beach
balanced on a pebble.

The ocean is the mother of us all.

Driving, he knew how to handle it,
This is going to take a long time, he sighed
and checked the rear view mirror of the car.

What Memories Are Carried In Light?

I have read it: the light Pablo Neruda saw adrift
in the Chilean Andes, sea and sun while bells rang an
ocean breeze. Jane Kenyon's golden dust sparkle of
late day hay light. Jack Gilbert's Greek sun
hammering rock and weed followed by brilliant white
truest under moonlight.

Light allows mental constructions not yet imagined,
even in sleep
we play cinemas of passion
and apocalypse churned
from the crevasse of our unconscious inside
an exploded universe. Music creates light in the dark;
I see across vast stretches of Canadian plains swept
with brushes of broken clouds that pass onward,
sweep the steppes
of Tibet and sift through snowy trees in far
northern Russia. All over the world, light
attaching to everything that can hold,
traveling from everything that reflects.

Unending fathoms light travels, passing to the center of
the mind not in the middle of our heads, the
deeper heart which doesn't beat in our chests.
A quality of light all my life, a vision, Mediterranean
sun illuminating stone architecture like Impressionist
paintings.

But it's both there and not there, a quality
inside the tonality. Turning my vision inside out, it's
an image neither dream nor memory.
But it's also a feeling, a nameless loss, abstract like a
future past— the light of Antibes
Nicolas de Stael cut onto canvas—
non-figurative impasto. All Edward Hopper wanted
was to paint sunlight
on the side of a house. That light is outside my life.

I've seen southern California beach light after rainfall,
San Francisco's autumn sea light, a soft gray hush on
Manhattan streets, morning orange New Mexico
desert. Northern plains late afternoon slants across
cornfields, through windbreaks of the prairie, barn
swallows at dusk, hollyhocks in the farm yard, red
wing blackbirds in the marshes.
Oregon's Pacific light felt closest
to my vision; the sun below the coastal range,
colossal trees caught the gold light in the high
branches. And it glowed rose-pink among the snow
tops of the Cascades. As evening descended in thin
haze that light felt distant from my life, too.

Catskill Mountains, blue stone origins from under the
sea, light's witness longer than ancient stories have
told, sunlight comes yellow through
the forest and falls into the lap of my yard
where it bathes all that I hold dear. Including you,

who hold the only way I have to tell you. Six p.m.
summer, the entire spectrum falling everywhere.
Flora and fauna of the wood wave and scramble,
gather up the day's diminishing light. It flows quick
nanoseconds while we perceive the slow subtleties.
Our eyes rise, lower, blink and we stretch our leaf of
skin up and outward.

—But it's late-August, my feet high in the dunes of
the cape, cool dry sand, sun down, glowing sea sky
twilight, a perfect calmness. Laughter, I am tan—
it's the most beautiful I've ever felt— but more; my
children, the color of bronze, shine a light
no tenderness could ever hold, for our hands
are too much sinew, tendons require a tension
from which light travels free as we leap, Earth
continues falling through space— gravity pulls
at our hearts, and we are left with a gentleness beyond
our bodies' possibility.

April

Elderly ladies need nourishment
and eat in diners where men are quiet
in between small talk in small towns.
The silence thins coffee collected
in white ceramic saucers. Their large
eyes search the periphery; they clutch
purses in their laps and button sweaters.
A sensible serving of pudding—
they save slices of pie for special
after church dinners when early dusk
settles in the tulip beds. Robins sing
from trees with no leaves. The ladies rest
in recliners nestled in dusted apartments,
ticking clocks sit on grandmother's
crocheted doilies. Glass figurines
wait in bright gift bags for the little girls.

October Gray

On the day you discover melancholy
in the third grade,

sidewalk puddles with foggy drizzle,
blurry lights fill school bus windows,
gray chalkboard, pencil lead,
even autumn leaves and crayons
don't have the same brightness,
you're too young to have a name for it.
The word *sad* is reserved
for the old dog who no longer retrieves the ball
and broken kite strings.

The mist holds something out there,
possibly far outside this town, some
thing you had once, but can't think of its name
or recall its shape.

Lost in this unclearness,
as the teacher talks addition and spelling,
you sense that sadness and longing
lay across your world like a heavy blanket,
keeps fog under skin. This subject
isn't discussed outside or inside
school and isn't on any map
scrolled up on the wall.

This incompleteness, separation,
like your life's distant future
momentarily grasped

where you sit chin in hand, already wistful
for a past that has yet to pass.
We are all born poets. However
most become economists.
In third grade the poets
find that something is missing,
and they love rain in October
even though it breaks their hearts
because they are sure what is lost
is out there calling them.

They search for words with which to answer back,
the words which will part the sky that has come
to Earth, and there in all the radiant glory of love
will be the key to it,

hummingbird of the soul,
true beating heart of hearts of hearts
engine of the matter.

Nice Clothes

The afternoon I left his side to get paperwork
        done back at the apartment,
I inexplicably took a sharp turn into the shopping
        center. I bought four

button-down oxfords, a nice pair of slacks and a
        European-cut blazer at a good price.
What was I doing? Shopping for things I didn't
        need, with money

I didn't have, in the middle of my dad's health care
        crisis. However, the next day,
my father unexpectedly died. It was quite clear
        then why I needed nice clothes.

There's no training for it, I'm thankful for the
        funeral *director* (did that make me
the *producer*?). So many details to think of on the
        same day he died. No plan,

just trying to suss out the desires of someone no
        longer able to wish. I made it up
as we went: announcements, service, epitaph,
        programs, coffin, clothes. Clothes?

Shouldn't we depart the way we arrived?
           Somehow, that doesn't feel appropriate,
but why not? Not Puritanism, more a sense of
           vulnerability to the elements.

His nephew suggested winter fishing wear: red
           and black checked wool shirt, wool pants
and wool socks, but that seems undignified, not to
           mention hot and itchy. My father was

fastidious about his appearance – haircut every
           two weeks, trim nails, shaved every day
including the day he died. He wore a suit and tie
           to the office five days a week. He

undressed after work with the same care. That
           was time for casual wear. I want him
to be comfortable and I think, it doesn't matter,
           but he would never think a funeral

anything less than a formal occasion. He'd been
           retired twenty years, but his work clothes still
hung in the closet. I picked out a black suit, a
           white shirt, blue and silver tie,

took the clothes to the dry cleaners. I dropped
           them off at the funeral home,
clean and pressed. Wait, one more question,
           socks and shoes? No, that feels wrong.

The feet should be bare, in touch with the earth.
    The feet bare,
like the hands and the face, for what is more
    uniquely ours?

Copper Memories

I stopped into a convenience store for a snack. A substantial snowfall lay on the streets and sidewalks. I had been shoveling all morning and I was hungry. The store, quite crowded, was out of nearly everything except batteries, shaving blades, pens. I paid for a milkshake. I noticed pennies scattered along the floor of the aisle near the empty food rack. I picked one up. It was a wheat penny, 1947. *I'll keep that one,* I thought and put it in my pocket. I picked up another and it was etched with a street sign, a street I used to live on in a distant city. *This is cool,* I said to myself, *I didn't know they made these.* I continued to pick up penny after penny each etched with a different scene: a mailbox, a lamppost illuminating falling snow, a Dutch elm tree, a crack in the sidewalk I always stepped over on my way to kindergarten, a stucco house, the corner five & dime I rode to on my tricycle. Each penny marked a place from my past. I walked to my car with a pocketful. The snow was piled high on the boulevard. I sipped my milkshake. There was still a lot of snow to shovel and a long way to go before I arrived at the next city.

It Is The 4th Of July, Again

The early morning has that moist, cool warmth
that I love, summer air with haze allows
me to stare at the low sun. I know it will be hot.
The thermals are unsettled. Two years ago,
my mom had a week left to live,
but my brother and I didn't know this.

The three of us awoke in her apartment
to hear the experimental physicists in Switzerland
announce they found the *God Particle,* the Higgs
Boson, but whether the universe exhibits
Supersymmetry or Chaos, they could not say—
as usual, after epiphany there are more questions.

My brother did the shopping: hot dogs, potato salad,
baked beans in molasses, ice cream, but the
store was out of hot dog buns. *Impossible,* I said, *it's
the 4th of July, the laws of supply
and demand will prevail!* He went
for a run in the heat of mid-day. I drove
to find buns for our junk-food franks—
empty shelves everywhere save those
full of hamburger buns. They'll do, they're buns,
but the imperfection bugged us. Televised fireworks
for mom and brother. Before I left
for the local display, my mom wrote a note
to my girls wishing them a happy 4th signed,
Hope it's a Bang!

*

The last note she ever wrote them. This morning the note is clear among the chaos of photos, cards, odd magnets and the current calendar posted to the refrigerator door.

Long-Legged Blond

She didn't jump down
from her crouch atop
the three-foot ledge.
Long haired, lithe human
leapt straight out—
unfolded her legs simply to the ground,
continued forward in one motion;
head never-changing height.
Twelve years old, chasing
the errant bouncing ball.

What I Wish

The moment the light flickers from my eyes,
I wish to find myself outdoors at a table
on the terrace of a street-level cafe
with a slice of my mother's cherry pie,
a cup of dark roasted coffee
lightened with fresh cream and, I suppose,
since I am dead to this world, a cigarette.
One which always gives the tobacco's first pull
of smoke across the mouth's roof
mixing with smooth Guatemalan Antigua
with its French roasted chocolate hint
creating an aroma rising through nasal passages
as it passes the back of the throat.

I will find myself alone. If you pass by
a simple nod, tip of the hat or smile will do.
I will watch the sunlight expand into shadows
like an opening blossom, the cobblestones
shine in a quiet back alleyway near a park
within sight or sound of ocean waves—
though a river, stream or fountain would be
enough for a melody of water to mix with bird song
in the trees. I will have with me
a book of poems, a notebook and a pen. Though what
book? *Refusing Heaven* or *God's Silence, Without End*
or *Let Evening Come?* Perhaps,
All of Us or *What The Living Do?* I will have

a stack of books. My ink will never run out
and my notebook will be blank and unruled.
All I will write is my name and the date.

Time doesn't exist though there is motion in the
leaves. My memories exist for me to access,
surrounded like a living picture book with sound,
smell, taste and touch to ripple through me and pass
on as I recall them. The years of age fourteen
and before interest me most. Individual days,
not just events that bleed together
into childhood. Was I more myself then—
who else could I be? Why did I stray from that boy
and did I ever return?

I will also contemplate whether or not
anything I ever said to my love was as meaningful
as observing the moonlight falling upon her hair?
Were the white feathers I saw float out of the blue
evidence of the soul's endurance? I will know or
not and smile. Of course, I'd do it all over again. Maybe
slight revisions, a couples of *Yeses*
instead of *No's* here and a *No thank you*
or two instead of *Why not's?* there, but honestly,
reliving one July afternoon of sandlot baseball
at nine-years-old might be enough for eternity.

I will leave my books and stroll along,
no particular direction. There is a gathering.
It's impossible to be late or to get lost. I will

be there. I don't know who else will attend,
but I look forward to philosophical debates
that end with the absurd, frivolity punctuated with
belly laughs and dancing which leaves our skin
steaming in the cool evening air. Like all parties that
must end, we depart with kisses
and go our separate ways to meet whatever may
        come next.

Shared Burden

Railroad cars are difficult to push
uphill especially
and with one's father no less,
rolling through covered bridges
that lie hidden behind doors
like garages (that do not open
automatically). Behind
each door a mystery of terrain,
but, surprisingly, we have
the strength to do it
over and over again,
though there is nothing
to mark our progress,
just another door
and dark, deep weeds
or desert behind it, our cargo
in front of us, passengers
faceless and nameless.
The hulking load moving slowly
but steadily,
by sweat of our will
toward some, no doubt,
unspectacular destination.

To Know The Difference

The impulse was to bury our father with meaning,
for the living, to embrace a generation
now passed. We told stories, said prayers
and played music. I got him the plain pine box
he always went on about and had him dressed
in a fine suit. Somebody suggested we bury
him with his favorite fishing rod, but I felt
that fine tool should be used to catch more fish.

He died at the facility. I collected
things quietly in the presence of his body.
Electric razor, tooth brush, clothes folded
in a dresser drawer. In his pants pocket,
a medallion from Alcoholics Anonymous—
the serenity prayer on the flip side.
I put it in my pocket. Thirteen years since he
stopped drinking. He did it to save his life
and get my mother back into the house. He went
to AA for 3 months then said, *What's the point of
continuing? Everybody tells their story
and you move on.*

We didn't talk about it. He didn't lecture us,
allowed others to drink in his home. He never
took another sip even after my mother
left for good seven years later. Alone in the house,
wife moved out of state, a son on each coast

and he in the middle. Who'd have blamed him if he
had? I thought his coin would steel me. Maybe
some luck if not fortitude in it. A touchstone.
But I hadn't found it in his jewelry box with cuff links
and rings, it was in the pocket of the pants
he wore to the hospital. He faced the end
with a wristwatch, $38 and his coin of humble prayer.

I wear the watch, the cash gone from his wallet,
but that coin, it wasn't mine. He earned it.
He came of age during the Great Depression,
hunted and fished for food. A Tech Sergeant
in World War II, he didn't fuck around or whine—
he just did what needed to be done. I wasn't going
to get that from a brass coin. The one I slipped into
his breast pocket the day we sent him on his way.

Last Meal

My father had been eating only ice cream
for a week since entering the facility,
refused everything else. This one afternoon
I was there when lunch was served: boneless
chicken breast, corn, mashed potatoes, gravy,
and apple cobbler with ice cream. I didn't expect
him to eat and I was hungry. He expressed
interest. His breath and arms too weak, I spread
a napkin across his hospital gown
and fed him. Grunts, nods and pointing
brought forkfuls to his mouth in desired order,
sips of water in between. He told me once, *I live
to eat.* I'm more of an *eat to live* type,
but I never went hungry as a child. He ate it all,
finished with dessert. I dabbed his chin,
happy that his appetite was back and maybe soon,
his strength. Sated, he slept through supper
I heard the next morning from the tall, strong
orderly, who assured me I needn't worry
about leaving before evening. I had been there
with him, he'd seen that
the day before.

Conveyance Object #4, 1976-1977

Ralph Humphrey

The day rises blue,
all blue, nothing else,
filling the space behind
and between things, space
that is not me or you. Space
that appears to be empty, it too
is blue. Other colors become
an end point for our sight: black
birds, red cars, a yellow house, green
hills, brown shoes, gray cement,
distract us from the veil of blue sky
between even our fingers, our eyelashes,
our parted lips. Blue things like teapots,
dinner plates, bluebirds and mailboxes double back
air and light in resonant waves of blue
becoming electric. When the death ship comes
to collect my soul, I wish to ride
the pure white sails clear into the cobalt blue
that must continue forever, deep,
deep plumb of the depths,
blue behind the blue that is bluer yet,
disappear into that sky full of nothing but itself.

III

What I Wanted To Tell You

While you are on vacation I am living on
beef stew and apple pie. The whip cream
thick. I make the regular pot of coffee
and realize the half left over is yours.
The dogs take their walks and hurry back
to be disappointed at the driveway with one car.
They look at me to explain your absence
or make you stride through the door.

It's good to know that the sun shines
where you are, as it does here, though
the light is different on the coast. You'll bring me
a sweatshirt from the sea side town: red
or blue or brown; I'll have a clean kitchen
and a fresh made bed. This distance
will be a memory. Summer's end flies
toward winter, but first leaves must fall. We'll
walk through those together. Out of the blue
this afternoon, migrating monarchs
begin filling our yard.

Why I Don't Write Like Frank O'Hara

We need more orange in our life,
you said out on Cape Cod. I agreed,
and we bought the coffee mugs,
discussed painting our bedroom cantaloupe.

Not garish, a cheerful,
healthy orange hue like the rose sky
reflecting off the low-tide beach, giving our skin
an Ivy League glow. Orange

is presumed a terrible color,
not as a poor choice for interior decoration,
but terrible as in painful for the soul
amidst the fierceness of life, orange

now meaning caution, hazard, warning
or way to find something, see plainly.
It's a squirt of citrus in the eye. I do think
that each life ought to have the color orange

in it and even some yellow, though that brings in
a tone too much to discuss alongside
orange, which is not subtle, no matter its shade.
It stands alone. It is not afraid. The color orange

should be revered. Yet, on those brilliant days
when our lives are most revealed, rays of sunlight
illuminating orange do make it too terrible,
like our trespasses borne out among the gray of
        the world.

Acceptance

We do all that we can
    of course
    without question
    it's what we do
    as people

we make calls
    handle affairs
    play music and read aloud
    induce laughter
    sit in the fullness of silence

we lift and carry
    raise water to lips
    apply cool washcloths
    stroke faces and hair

say, *It's OK, there are oceans of love*
    shores of forgiveness

we can provide

but we cannot perform
the miraculous
and that is what makes us
moan, whimper, bewildered
crawl and cry.

Invisible

On a walk in the neighborhood
the smell of opened flesh
like field-dressed, gutted prey
greeted me bright early winter Sunday.
Sometime before dawn, the hunted,
haunted by a gaining death whose angry,
spitting, swinging wooden arms
splintered the dirty crusted snow, fell
and laid still with labored breathing.

Burgundy blood, chalky glaciers
congealed by icy city sidewalks. I stand
at a spot where only hours before
a terrified soul, its grieving grip
beaten loose from bruised flesh,
swelled, floated through the sharp
bare branches of February. The only
marker, high atop the Dutch elm,
a gleaming silver helium balloon
snagged by an arching branch,
HAPPY BIRTHDAY.

Faith

Crystals hung in the blind-
darkened windows turn slowly
without light. They used to spray
morning rainbows along the walls,
bright glints of sun on floor and ceiling.

The hum and whir of the oxygen converter
steady pulse night and day. Low
bubble of water for humidity
in the tube which snakes across the floor,
the sleeping woman slumped
to her left, pillows propped against
the set of drawers next to the recliner.
The lights above the stove and bathroom sink
remain on. She gathers the energy
to rise for her needs and then back to the chair
to rest until the next event.

Hum and whir — first day of spring, Easter,
birthday, Mother's Day — no change.
The blinds stay drawn,
the door closed and unlocked.
Weight and strength do not arrive.

The darkness has permanently
colored the walls with blackness
like smoke. Fear is in the corners
and under the furniture. It is not
heavy, but does not sweep away.

This is somebody's life, a vessel
of history. Light and love still in the eyes
she hungers for the spiritual end.
Cut flowers bright in the vase
like prayers for the future
when things might be, will be,
better. Somebody is beside her, here, now.

The Hands Of My Mother

Sharp, she cannot speak, but writes on a dry erase
board with exquisite penmanship. Handwriting
learned in the one-room schoolhouse. Seeing her in
the hospital bed, it is her hands that I cannot
comprehend. My mother's father,

six foot, two inches tall, Alsatian, a farmer
who hitched his Belgian horses to plow the fields
with hands strong as Earth, lifted his little girl.
My hands, large enough to palm a basketball
when they were young, full of strength, now
lift my mother to sit her upright. The body
with tubes and wires, too frail for the world pulsing in
the street down below. Her hands, dexterous with the
intricate lines and swirls
of language, communicate what her tongue

no longer permits. The hospital staff marvel
to read her thoughts as if they've forgotten how—this
dry erase board with black marker
the link between stone tablet and tablet computer.
She directs the air with simple sign language: *OK*—
thumbs up; a touch to the heart- *Thank you*;
a kiss blown with two fingers after touching the
heart — *Thank you and bless you*;

palms out and up-turned— a shrug; a slice through
air— *Stop* or *No*; one forefinger raised–
a pause. The strength still in her hands

when she hasn't the strength to raise her head. Her
hands look able to fly,
migrate to any place willing to embrace her. Though
her long, slender fingers played piano, these are not
hands of aristocracy, these are hands of labor, able to
handle work with finesse;
administer needles when she was a nurse, type 110
words a minute, mend clothing, cut up a chicken,
wield a wooden spoon like a baton. Her hands which
used to lift me. Now I know where

mine have come from and I see them in their final
beauty. The nurses, doctors and technicians
come and go, make notes in a binder, a chart of
equations: heart rate, oxygen level, blood pressure,
potassium, CC's, IV's
and milliliters; all measurements adding up
to a life in a bed going one way or another. Nobody
notices that her hands have become
shining doves carrying us all on wings of salt,
conducting a symphony we cannot measure,
an opera of what becomes erased.

Second Influence

There was no love from the man
or the woman in the garden,
there was only nakedness. Pure in their nature—
no more, no less, no happiness, no ambition,
no fear. Sleep under the blaze of heaven, gaze

sweet in the shine of the sun,
even the river tasted of honey
and the bees never stung. Not necessary
to declare one thing for another as all
was level, eye to eye. But the story

tells that there were two others
in the garden, both born of power.
One filled with love
and one filled with pride.

They each bore their gift;
one to give life, the other
to give knowledge of life.
How were the innocent
ever to know the difference?

What Was Left At The End

Stories, his 1920's childhood. A bully threw mud into brother Dick's eyes. Eldest sister, Hazel, washed out the sting with Des Moines River water. He and a friend, a girl, swam across the river and ate their fill of green apples. They headed back too soon, he cramped up halfway, sidestroke, she swam him to shore to save his life. Cats use their whiskers to judge the size of openings, whether or not to enter. The kittens, whose whiskers he'd cut off, squeezed through a crack in the porch's foundation. Never saw them again, worried the damage he'd done. Preceded in death by brother and sister, last of that generation, he was now gasping for what surrounds us. He shook my hand, firm as his word, brown eyes clear as autumn sunlight, *Thanks for coming, son.* I left the radio tuned to the game. Later, all he had to do was press the 'on' button. I didn't hear him speak again. Leaving the life to be written by somebody else, he passed through his stories sometime in the night. I reach into the river.

Maybe In My Eyes

Late-July flowers: pink, orange, yellow, white
surround the shade of the portico;
sun on stone driveway breeze in oak leaves.
I think of my mother who used to exist,
myself a child, not long ago.
I realize language can't say it.

What I want to say is on the other side of
thought— region of intangibility. It's the sum
of these parts on this specific day. Even a 3D motion
picture, precise sound,
would not convey it—

for it is only me, my love,
my own sense of time's vastness and minute
treasures— *here*, at the meeting point where
I exist in space and time ceases to exist at all,
I speak to you and say nothing,
a hollow mouth. Only the high hawk
of archetypal light can see the formless,
waving in the meadow.

Astonishment

Only we can burn our own hearts
at the proper temperature.

A requirement of transgressions against
our individual consciousness. Yet,

it is human nature to act against
our will, our iron discipline, our firm
personal beliefs, even when we know.

There is a weakness not composed
of character, but built into the flesh
that desires sensation when
face to face with aging and death.

Bat Dream

When you awake to find
your arms covered in bats
do not panic. There may be
forty beady-eyed mammals
with sharp teeth crawling under
the sleeves of your night shirt,
but they have warm, fuzzy, fur bodies.
They've been watching you
all your life coming and going
in your more or less unchanged
routines. If they could, with their
little suckling mouths, they would
say, *It's time for a change, that's all.*
So, rise from your bed,
hold your fear under your skin,
gently, but quickly step outside,
raise your arms in the burgeoning dawn
and let them go. Let them lift off
and if necessary, it's ok
to give your arms a little shake,
a little shimmy, to get the last few bats
out from under your sleeves.
They'll be grateful, you'll be ready.
Close your eyes then; you can hear
the spirits whisper and sigh.

Air Travel

Don't we all want to leave something behind,
if not a legacy, a center for education
or a hospital wing, at least our last words
charred but readable in a notebook pulled
from the dying embers of an airliner? Or the last
words carried to a loved ones' ears upon
the last breath. Even last words to a stranger
might be enough if they are memorable—
not for being your last but for helping the living
carry the torch of life.

There are many things to leave behind,
stuff to be dispersed or tossed. People want
to leave money and valuables, but like those
words, they're fleeting like time spent
on this hard rock made of temporary light. What
can we take with us? Certainly not what we
are buried with: rings, watches, clothes, pets,
books or coins on our eyes. But perhaps
we take other people's wishes, fears,
anger, and love. And those emotions
that we leave behind, do those burdens
and treasures eventually dissipate in time's
long shadow across the heavens?

Surviving

for: M.P.

You wake at an odd time of morning,
say 2:46 A.M. You fell asleep on the couch.
The modem's light is blinking and it's in synch
with the tick of the kitchen clock's second hand.
A car drives by slowly on the road, its light
swings across the living room wall,
seconds later another slowly moving automobile,
you think maybe they are stopping
at your driveway and wonder why,
who? There is a *scrape* and *clomp*,
scrape and *clomp*
under the sink. You had set a trap there
and indeed something is trapped
behind the cabinet doors.

You get a flashlight, not wanting to
flood the rooms of the sleeping with brightness.
Slinking around your own dark house
makes you feel suspicious, like a burglar,
like somebody could be watching you—
but what's on your mind
is the dream of death from which you awoke.
A couple in love, but the woman jumped
into the water and drowned, the man wept
through the rest of the dream and you
waded into the water, a brilliant yellow
butterfly floated just under the surface.

You scooped it up, water running
through your fingers. What a wonder! A butterfly,
whole, underwater, you let it go into the air.

This dream began with a giant kid, glasses,
blond hair, squishing people in the streets
with a single press of his forefinger. You hid
near a tree. Was this the new image of death?
Instead of cloak, scythe, and cold,
bony hand; shaggy hair, striped shirt,
buck teeth and pudgy finger squishing
people like ants. Funny perhaps,
but as one of the ants— terrifying. Fleeing
brought you to the river's edge
where the couple stood just before their tragedy.
But at three o'clock in the morning what's really
on your mind is the actual death of a friend
a few days earlier. He jumped off a bridge.
The river took him whole.

Opening the cabinet doors the persistent
scrape and *clomp* is clear, a mouse
partly in the spring trap. The metal
bar across its lower back, front claws trying
to get somewhere. You were warned
about this very thing happening. You set it
anyway. Most of the time it finishes
in silence. Your grandparents, your parents,
would have finished this pest without thought.

It's a mouse, for Christ's sake, the cats catch them
and you turn your back.
What makes this different you cannot say.

Broken back, front half still working for life.
Like the rope breaking, surviving the fall,
providence setting one free, sort of. You pick it up,
take it outdoors to the edge of woods, lift the bar.
The paraplegic mouse pulls itself forward,
crawling into the night leaves. You are guilty
of something, but don't understand what to feel.
You will sleep again tonight. In the morning light
you will try to forget the mouse.
Picture him whole and living.

Prayer

I leave the now sleeping revelers
and walk alone into fields under the first spires
of light. I fall to my knees hidden
by prairie grasses and wildflowers wet with dew,
liquids flowing from my face.
I am balling so hard the spiders hide
in their glistening webs. I apologize
to open sky, witness of every breath,
having so much love for every thing
that dares to sweetly unfold its heart
I am choking and must pour
it out into my homeland. I am
thankful to be here among my tribe,
but I cannot give enough to feel worthy
of my blessings. I am not ready to die.
I want to explode, a star of pure light,
sear even the souls of stones
with this love, then no longer be a me,
but a forgotten piece of morning instead,
melting into the golden August earth
like a voice clear in a ripple of water.

Guy Reed is author of the chapbooks, *The Effort To Hold Light* (Finishing Line Press), *Still Life With Acorn* (Fool Head Press), and co-author, with Cheryl A. Rice, of *Until The Words Came* (Post Traumatic Press). He's published in journals, anthologies and read his work on the podcast, *The Strange Recital*. He contributed 2 poems and performed one, in a featured role for the film, *I Dream Too Much* (The Orchard). A Minnesota native, Guy's lived in California, Oregon and currently resides in the Catskill Mountains with his wife and their children.